# CHESAPEAKE
## PORTS OF CALL & ANCHORAGES

By Thomas A. Henschel
Aerial Photography by Lucien F. Miner
Editor & Contributor • James A.M. Johnston

CHESAPEAKE

Published by Mile High Publishing & Graphics, Waynesville, NC

## PUBLISHED BY

**Mile High Publishing & Graphics**
323 Hyacinth Drive
Clyde, NC 28721
Tel. & Fax 828-627-9104
Toll Free:1-888-818-6640
Web Site: www.chesapeakebound.com
www.abacobound.com
E-Mail: thlp@earthlink.net

---

## DISTRIBUTED BY

**Cruising Guide Publications**
P.O. Box 1017
Dunedin, Florida 34697-1017
Phone: (800) 330-9542 • (727) 733-5322
Fax: • (727) 734-8179
Web Site: www.cruisingguides.com • E-Mail: infocruisingguides.com

By **THOMAS A. HENSCHEL**
**Publisher**

**AERIAL PHOTOGRAPHY**
Lucien F. Miner

**ASSOCIATE PUBLISHER**
Lee Marie Pischedda

**EDITOR & CONTRIBUTOR**
James A.M. Johnston

**DEDICATION**
*This book is dedicated in loving memory of Robert (Robbie) Pischedda.*
*Rather than wanting much in life, he touched and gave more to others.*

First Edition
ISBN 0-9704068-1-9

Historic Concord Point Lighthouse at Havre de Grace -- Photo Tom Henschel

# Where the Countryside meets the Chesapeake

## Herrington Harbour North

Lat 38.45.86 / Long 76.32.80

Located on Herring Bay • www.herringtonharbour.com

1-800-297-1930

# CONTENTS

Baltimore's Inner Harbor -- Photo Tom Henschel

## THE CHESAPEAKE

Why do I love the Chesapeake I am asked?
As I stare into a fire one cold evening deep in the Smoky Mountains.
Why do I love the Chesapeake, I ponder.
Where do I start -- how do I answer -- or is there an answer?
Is it watching the watermen plying their trades on a cool morning or
Seeing the laughing gulls stalking a school of menhaden?
Is it watching the tides flow and ebb while sitting on an empty dock or
Listening to the migrant loons chortling over food unseen with the naked eye?
Why do I love the Chesapeake, I ponder.
My mind returns to memories of a month's sail on the Bay.
Sailing -- perhaps that is the tie -- that is the draw.
Is it the joy one feels battling down the Bay into a southwest wind or
Waking up in a snug harbor with frost on the deck?
Is it seeing the morning light glint off the masts of silent sloops or
Hearing the winds rattling the rigging late at night?
Why do I love the Chesapeake, I ponder.
Is it the Bay's history -- which is a history of America:
St. Mary's, St. Michaels, Oxford, Annapolis, and Cambridge or
Seeing the skipjacks under full sail bringing back a forgotten age?
Is it hearing church bells breaking the stillness of a foggy morning or
Realizing the ties which bond man and the Chesapeake remain unbroken?
Why do I love the Chesapeake, I am asked?
I stare into the fire, silent, as there is no clear answer to give.

**by James A.M. Johnston**

Oxford looking to the southeast.

# INTRODUCTION

*by James A.M. Johnston*

Approximately 800 miles north of the Florida coast and an equal distance south of Casco Bay, Maine lies one of the largest watershed basins or estuaries in the United States: the Chesapeake Bay. The Bay, in its entirety, covers 64,000 square miles in three states; Delaware, Maryland, and Virginia. It receives millions of gallons of fresh water from 150 rivers and their tributaries including the Susquehanna, Potomac, Rappahannock, York, Choptank, and Chester, which makes it one of the most important ecological regions on the Eastern Seaboard.

For the mariner searching for a boater's paradise where the seasons are long and the weather mild, the Chesapeake should be at the top of the list of places to visit. The Bay offers the more adventurous mariner a unique opportunity to anchor and enjoy secluded harbors and inlets along most of its navigable waters. And yet, for those who prefer the more active life docked at well run marinas with restaurants, stores, showers, and power hookups there are many worth visiting.

The Chesapeake is easy to reach by water. From the north, the C&D canal, built in 1829, is the simplest route and connects the Delaware River with the upper reaches of the Bay and the charming Chesapeake City which offers an excellent anchorage along the canal.

From the south, one can take the Intracoastal Waterway (ICW) to Norfolk, Virginia at the southwestern corner of the Bay. As Norfolk is a naval base, there is a lot of shipping activity and care should be taken. Norfolk also has numerous bridges; some having clearances under 12 feet. Many have limited, opening schedules and the boater would be advised to schedule his passage accordingly.

Norfolk is a convenient stop with excellent marinas, restaurants, and sights as is nearby Hampton.

For those bluewater sailors wanting to travel on less protected waters, the Bay can be reached from the Atlantic. When travelling on these outside routes, paying attention to regional weather reports is a must.

The Maryland and Virginia communities found on the Bay, are steeped in American history and to this day, maintain a flavor reminiscent of America's past. Many communities were founded in the early 1600's by Europe-

*A sculpture honoring Chesapeake watermen in the Annmarie Gardens on Saint John in Solomons Island.*

Photo Tom Henschel

ans who left their native lands to escape religious prosecution or for a desire to improve their lives in a new land. Certainly most of you are familiar with Jamestown, but many do not know that communities along the Bay proper were being established throughout the same period.

A large majority of the sites outlined, in *The Chesapeake Bay Ports of Call and Anchorages*, are communities with long histories and strong ties to the Bay. Tangier and Smith Islands are examples which have been able to maintain a lifestyle and culture not found anywhere else on the Bay or the United States. These islands have been isolated from the mainland for centuries and only recently has the outside world discovered them. Consequently, if you have an opportunity to visit these islands in your travels, it will feel as though you have stepped back in time.

North of the Potomac River, at the mouth of the Patuxent River, is Solomons Island, another favorite, cruising port of call. With outstanding marinas, a protected harbor, dining, shopping, and quiet anchorages, it is a destination that should be placed on any itinerary.

Continuing north along the Western Shore is Herring Bay, which offers some of the Chesapeake's largest and finest marinas. Herrington Harbour North, at the northern end of the bay, has one of the most extensive facilities for yacht maintenance and service.

Above Herring Bay, you pass the South and West Rivers before reaching Annapolis, Maryland. This city is home to the U. S. Naval Academy and is the present state capital. It is a bustling city offering an abundance of eateries and opportunities to walk along the waterfront or its adjacent, side streets. If you want a beautiful evening stroll, head up

*Continued on Page 12*

Rock Hall -- The Haven

"It looks like a country club, yet we are a serious working boatyard."

*--Jonathan Jones, General Manager*

*A forsaken dream.*

*Continued from Page 9*

from the waterfront to view the spectacularly lit Capitol Building. For the boater, Annapolis also is the site of two, annual boat shows in the fall. One is specifically designed for powerboat enthusiasts and the other, for those who rely on the wind.

At the further, northern reaches of the Bay is Baltimore. Being a larger city, it has a greater variety of shops, restaurants and amusements. The highlight of your visit to this city is touring the recently restored Inner Harbor waterfront. When visiting Baltimore, however, a few hours should be saved to travel the short distance by water taxi to Fell's Point with its historic downtown.

Leaving the Western Shore and heading to the eastern side of the Bay at the Bay Bridge is Kent Narrows. Both the Bay Bridge area and Kent Narrows have been and remain appealing to the Chesapeake's boaters as they feature numerous, fine marinas and a variety of dining options and activities.

Loosely translated into English from the Algonquin (Native American) language, "Chesapeake" is the " Great Shellfish Bay " and it continues to live up to its reputation. Consequently, its maritime history revolves around the watermen who, for centuries have harvested the bounty of these waters. An Eastern Shore town with long ties to the fishing industry is St. Michaels, which is now, home to the Chesapeake Bay Maritime Museum (CBMM).

Similar to Mystic Seaport in Mystic, Connecticut, the CBMM is a working museum. As such, it gives its visitors the unusual opportunity to witness professional ship- wrights actually restoring old vessels previously used in the fishing industry. The museum also has slips available for members at discount rates.

Approximately 30 miles, or a comfortable day's sail, south of St. Michaels is the town of Oxford, which also has a rich and colorful maritime connection. Main Street

is lined with stately houses and its ferry service is one of the oldest continuously running ferries in the country. Oxford is extremely small. Although there are ample marinas with maintenance facilities, slips for travelling boaters and several great spots to anchor, there is only one store. This could be a drawback if one is hoping to fully restock the larder. The store is well run and does have a good selection of fresh breads, wine, beer, and adequate groceries to tide one over. For the nature lover, Oxford and its environs happens to be on the flyway for a variety of waterfowl. During the early fall, when the algae blooms have died off, it is a favorite stop for common loons heading south.

Heading north up the eastern shoreline from Oxford

*The Chesapeake Bay boasts some of the country's finest marinas.*

and St. Michaels, is the Chester River, one of the major river systems entering the Chesapeake Bay. Approxi- mately 18 miles up the Chester is Chestertown, founded in the late 1600's and home to Washington College. The river is wide and offers excellent anchoring, and there are two small marinas, which have slips for boaters passing through. Historically, Chestertown was on the major south/north route used by the opposing armies during the Revolutionary War and General George Washington was a frequent visitor. Chestertown has, through the centu- ries, managed to maintain much of its old charm and a stroll down Main Street and its adjacent, side streets is a must.

After re-entering the Chesapeake from the Chester River and continuing north, the first town, Rock Hall, has long been a boater's paradise. As its harbor is small and very popular during the boating season, any visitor

coming by water should call ahead for a slip.

A good day's sail north along the Eastern Shore finds the mariner at the mouth of the Sassafras River. If your destination is the C&D Canal and points north, Georgetown, approximately seven miles up the Sassafras, is a perfect destination for a night as it is a short hop to the canal entrance. The Sassafras has an array of good anchorages and if you choose to anchor, you would not be alone. If you are able to get a mooring in Georgetown on a summer weekend, occasionally, you may be ser- enaded until the early hours by a variety of musicians on the shore.

*Editor's Note:* Using his popular book on Abaco, *The Bahamas -- Abaco Ports of Call & Anchorages*, as a template, Tom Henschel has created *Chesapeake Bay Ports of Call and Anchorages* for the boating community and visiting cruisers. Unlike many other informational books written about the Chesapeake, Henschel has taken a different approach - aerial photographs of various harbors com- bined with descriptive texts for each destination. Each destination is presented in a coffee-table format and is designed to be used in conjunction with other guides and charts of the Bay. As the Chesapeake is an enormous area to cover in one volume, the ports of call were chosen because of their diverse characteristics, varying attrac- tions, and their popularity among the cruising commu- nity.

Although not to be used for navigational purposes, the full page, color photographs with accompanying over- views depicting approaches and points of interest are invaluable as references. The extremely readable descrip- tion accompanying each photograph is a solid overview of the site's characteristics and gives the casual reader, the boating enthusiast, or the traveler an excellent resource to plan his own trip or cruise to the Chesapeake Bay.

*James A. M. Johnston, a wildlife biologist by profession, spends much of his free time sailing around the Chesapeake Bay in his 1948, Hinckley sloop,* Uncas.

*The* Constellation *in Baltimore's Inner Harbor.*

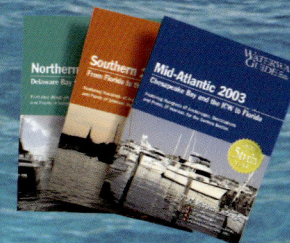

# There are seventeen shoals pictured here.

We tell boaters like you how to avoid them.
Since 1947, our cruise guides have covered the North East coast, the Chesapeake Bay,
the Intracoastal Waterway from Norfolk to Miami, and the American Gulf Coast.
Our goal for the past 56 years? Setting the standard for accuracy and on-the-water usability.
If your float plan includes our coverage areas—and you want expert advice
on the best marinas, the finest anchorages and the
safest routes—your helm station should include Waterway Guide.
Fully updated and redesigned for 2003.

## WATERWAY GUIDE
THE CRUISING AUTHORITY

# CHESAPEAKE CITY, MD

U.S. Army Corps Of Engineers & Museum

Engineer's Cove

Chesapeake Inn & Marina

SOUTH CHESAPEAKE CITY

City Dock

Chesapeake City Bridge

To Delaware

C & D Canal

To Elk River

NORTH CHESAPEAKE CITY

Bulkhead Dockage

Schaefer's Canal House & Marina

N

NOT TO BE USED FOR NAVIGATION
Use as a reference only. Consult
recommended charts for navigation.

The city docks to starboard entering the basin offers free dockage for a 24-hour period.

## ASHORE

Schaefer's Canal House and Marina in North Chesapeake City is well known among cruising boaters and yachtsmen since its establishment in 1908. It has long been a favorite destination along the canal because of its marina facilities and an outstanding restaurant. The marina provides dockage along a bulkhead and can accommodate the largest of yachts. In fact, if you are that fortunate to have your own helicopter, there is even a helipad adjoining the marina. Free dockage is available for restaurant patrons and entertainment is regularly scheduled. Besides providing a full-service marina, a market, ship's store and fuel, Schaefer's offers overnight accommodations in five nearby bed and breakfast establishments.

Across the C&D in South Chesapeake City, boaters will find the Chesapeake Inn Restaurant & Marina, located just after entering the anchorage basin. On the southern shore of the canal you will discover many points of interest, several restaurants, and other B&B's. There are several shops and other sights in this interesting and charming community and for the history fan, a visit to the C&D Canal Museum should be on your list of stops.

The Chesapeake & Delaware Canal, representing a colossal engineering feat with its opening in 1829, is a major shipping lane of the Intracoastal Waterway system, connecting the Chesapeake and Delaware Bays. Stretching 13 miles, it is important to both commercial and recreational traffic. The canal was constructed and is currently maintained by the U.S. Army Corps of Engineers.

For anyone transiting the C&D Canal, Chesapeake City should be considered as a port of call not to be passed by. The city is actually divided into Chesapeake North and South by the canal, and each offers its own special attractions.

## NAVIGATION

While the C&D Canal is well marked at the end of each entrance and navigation is straightforward, a sharp eye is key to its safe navigation because of the large ships and barge traffic sharing the waterway with much smaller craft.

A healthy current within the canal is another factor to consider. Reportedly, at times, the current can reach several knots, and this may greatly influence any docking maneuvers.

An anchorage capable of accommodating a small fleet of boats is found on the southern shore of South Chesapeake City near the U.S. Corps of Engineers base and the city dock. Here you will find depths of approximately 10 feet and, at most times, plenty of room for swinging at anchor.

Photo by Tom Henschel

*The anchorage at South Chesapeake City.*

# HAVRE DE GRACE, MD

NOT TO BE USED FOR NAVIGATION
Use as a reference only. Consult
recommended charts for navigation.

Tome's Landing

MacGregor's
Restaurant

Tidewater Grille

HAVRE DE GRACE

Tidewater Marina

Long Pond
Marina

N

small boat traffic, it is usually busy. The upside is that the channels are well marked. However, care should be taken to stay within the channel as there is shallow water on both sides. Consult your charts.

## ASHORE

For those of you who are looking for transient slips, Havre de Grace has several options. Below the first bridge on the western shore is the Havre de Grace Marina at Log Pond, Penn's Beach Marina and the Tidewater Marina. The Tidewater Grille, Vandiver Inn, Price's Seafood, The Crazy Swede, Bayou Restaurant, Happy's Snack Bar, Fortunato Brother Pizza and MacGregor's are among your restaurant choices and are within walking distance. Above the railroad bridge, on the eastern shore is Tome's Landing Marina, which does not have transient slips but does have a restaurant, basic marine supplies and fuel.

This community is the home of the Havre de Grace Decoy Museum which, at first glance may seem strange. However, the mouth of the Susquehanna River is extremely popular among waterfowl hunters and hunting has played a role in its cultural history. Along with the decoy museum is the Susquehanna Museum of HDG, Inc., the Havre de Grace Maritime Museum, the Steppingstone Museum, the Skipjack *Martha Lewis* and the paddlewheeler *Lantern Queen* which offer cruises.

The Susquehanna River is one of the major tributaries of the Chesapeake Bay travelling southeast through New York and Pennsylvania, and entering the Bay at Havre de Grace. Havre de Grace has played a major part in American History specifically the Revolutionary War, and its immediate aftermath and the War of 1812. Here, George Washington rested on his trips between his estate in Virginia and Philadelphia during the years prior to his becoming president, and it was well known to such historical figures as General Lafayette. During the War of 1812, the British attacked and burned the town to the ground, however, it still has been able to maintain vestiges of its historic past.

Because of its location, its solid historical flavor and its marina facilities, attractions, restaurants, and shops, Havre de Grace and the neighboring town of Perrysville are worthy of a visit.

## NAVIGATION

Havre de Grace is well marked by the 1827 Concord Point Lighthouse, which although no longer operating remains in place and is a present day tourist attraction having been recently restored. Once in the river, the most obvious landmark is Garrett Island, which is divided by two, fixed bridges. As the Susquehanna River is a major tributary and is open to shipping, commerce, and

*Downtown Havre de Grace.*

Photo Tom Henschel

# BALTIMORE, MD

Ravens Stadium · Camden Yards · World Trade Center · BALTIMORE INNER HARBOR · Inner Harbor Marina · Inner Harbor East Marina · Beach · Harbor View Marina · Domino Sugar · Main

NOT TO BE USED FOR NAVIGATION
Use as a reference only. Consult
recommended charts for navigation.

## ASHORE

The Inner Harbor has more shops and restaurants than can practically be listed here. Virtually any type of cuisine is available ranging from the finest gourmet fare to hot dogs and hamburgers. While the emphasis is on fun and entertainment, there are numerous other attractions you will want to visit. They include the Baltimore Maritime Museum on Pier 3, the B&O Railroad Museum, the Fire Museum of Maryland and the Maryland Science Center. No first time visit would be complete without a stop at the National Aquarium.

There are several options for dockage with walking access to the harbor including the Harbor View Marina, the Inner Harbor East Marina and the City of Baltimore Docks. Regardless of your location in this area, you can always hop aboard a water taxi and ride the entire day for a nominal, onetime fee, and drop offs and pickups are scattered throughout the city.

Baltimore, as one of the country's largest seaports, has additionally become increasingly attractive to the recreational boater. This has been due to a continuing revitalization of the downtown waterfront area which has been ongoing for the past two decades. The redevelopment has included the establishment of the immensely popular Inner Harbor complex.

Several modern marinas are located within walking distance of the many sights, cultural events and activities that this city has to offer. Any visiting boater cannot plan on taking it all in during a day's stay, or even touching the surface on a weekend cruise. Boaters who are sports fans have the opportunity to take in either a baseball game at Camden Yards to the see the Baltimore Orioles, or a professional football game at a new stadium watching the NFL Baltimore Ravens.

## NAVIGATION

Because of Baltimore's importance as a port, you can usually expect a great deal of ship traffic. These vessels are likely to be extremely large and caution should be utilized when travelling the shipping lanes. The Inner Harbor is entered through a deep and wide waterway that passes under the immense Francis Scott Key Bridge and by the historic Fort McHenry. You can expect the waterways and the harbor to be busy on any fair-weather weekend.

Photo Lucien F. Miner

*The Power Plant complex with an ESPN Zone, Barnes & Noble and Hard Rock Cafe taken from the Top of the World at the World Trade Center.*

# FELL'S POINT & CANTON, MD

Harborview Marina

Inner Harbor

Inner Harbor East Marina

NOT TO BE USED FOR NAVIGATION
Use as a reference only. Consult recommended charts for navigation.

FELL'S POINT & CANTON

Beach

City Pier At Fell's Point

Henderson's Wharf Marina & Inn

Anchorage Marina

Baltimore Marine Center

## ASHORE

Major marinas, which have transient slips available include the Anchorage Marina, the Baltimore Marine Center, Canton Cove Marina, Hendersons' Wharf Marina, Brown's Wharf Marina and the Bay View Marina.

A day or a night on the town is a must and most of the attractions, restaurants (and there are many reflecting different cuisine), and shops are within walking distance. Little Italy with a variety of eateries is nearby. Fell's Point also hosts two theaters; the Fell's Point Corner Theatre, which is located in the 1859 Fire House, presents many worthy " off Broadway " plays, and the Vagabond Players perform on Fridays and Sundays throughout the year at "On the Square " on South Broadway.

For those who want an historic bent to their visit, there is the Robert Long House, the London Coffee House, the Frederick Douglas Park and Marine Railway, and the Broadway Market, which has been in operation since the 1780's.

For the shopper, Fell's Point is known for its antique stores, boutiques, and craft shops to peruse through as well as a large number of restaurants with varied fare to sample. Overall, Fell's Point and Canton offer a wide range of attractions and activities.

Like many other seafaring harbors on the Bay, Fell's Point and the Canton areas are rich in maritime history and these cities have continued to maintain their many cultural and architectural ties to the past. Unlike Baltimore proper you will find that modern skyscrapers and glass have not dwarfed the architecture which exists and much of the area appears today as it did 300 years ago.

Although not the earliest settlement in Maryland, the history of Fell's Point dates back to approximately 1670. It wasn't until the mid 1700's, however, that Fell's Point came to the forefront as being a shipbuilding center with a deep water harbor to allow for commercial activities.

William Fell, who developed one of the first shipbuild-ing yards on the Patapsco River, initiated its jump into prominence. His son continued to build his father's business and within a short time, Fell's Point became known for the ships which were built there, as well as for being a major trading port.

## NAVIGATION

If you have entered the channel heading into Balti-more proper, entering Fell's Point on the Patapsco River is not difficult. The channel is well marked and as indicated in the previous section, there is plenty of water. As Fell's Point is still a major, busy harbor, anchoring is not recommended. However, there are ample marinas, which do have transient slips available.

*A flea market in Fell's Point town square.*

Photo by Tom Henschel

# ANNAPOLIS, MD

Severn River
U.S. Naval Academy
Annapolis City Dock
ANNAPOLIS
Navy Yard
N
Spa Creek Bridge
Petrini Shipyard
Spa Creek

NOT TO BE USED FOR NAVIGATION
Use as a reference only. Consult
recommended charts for navigation.

you will not run out of are potential places to tie up. Both sides of the creek are crowded with marinas not counting yacht clubs, town landings, ship stores and shipyards.

For transient dockage, choose from the Annapolis City Dock, the Annapolis Waterfront Marriott or the Yacht Basin Company. Reservations for dockage are suggested before setting out for this city. The Spa Creek area and Back Creek offer many more options.

One problem you will have in deciding what to do in Annapolis is determining how much time you have to spend. There are some obvious highlights. Annapolis is the home of the U. S. Naval Academy and St. John's College and a visit to these sites should be on your agenda. If you like historic buildings, there are many to choose from including: the Bruce House, the Charles Carol Barrister House, Chase-Lloyd House, the City Hall, the Courthouse, the Governor's Mansion, the old Treasury, and others. All can be reached by foot and there is actually a streetmap available to help you along.

Annapolis is home to the two major boat shows held in October of each year. The sailboat show is held first and then followed by the powerboat show.

A nyone visiting the Bay, especially by boat, should not miss an opportunity to visit this city which is rich in maritime and colonial history. Anne Arundel Town, now called Annapolis, was founded in 1649. By 1695, it had become the capital of Maryland and remains so to this day.

Throughout its history, Annapolis has been closely tied to the Bay. During its early years through the Revolutionary War period, it was the marine center for all types of commerce, culture and politics and, in many ways, remains so today. In fact, the ties to the Bay and the boating world have only increased, as it has become the undisputed Mecca for recreational boaters.

Unlike many other cities in Maryland and Virginia

which have suffered through wars and fires, Annapolis still has many beautiful examples of Georgian, Federal, Victorian, and modern architectural styles and a walk through the city, especially the historic district, is a must.

## NAVIGATION

Entering Annapolis is simple once you have reached the mouth of the Severn River. As with most ports of call on the Bay, the channel into Annapolis is well-marked, but if you have any questions or concerns, check your guides and charts.

## ASHORE

As Annapolis is the sailing center on the Bay, what

*Downtown Annapolis with the state capital in background.*

Photo Tom Henschel

# EASTPORT, MD

Severn River
Spa Creek
J World
Bert Jabin's Eastport
Mears Marina
Back Creek
EASTPORT & BACK CREEK
Port Annapolis Marina
Bert Jabin's Yacht Yard
N

NOT TO BE USED FOR NAVIGATION
Use as a reference only. Consult recommended charts for navigation.

## ASHORE

In the Eastport area, you have a number of marinas, which have space or slips for transient sailors. As with those marinas found in Spa Creek, these marinas may be very full during the height of the sailing season and anyone interested in staying in Back Creek for a night should make reservations. The larger marinas include the Port Annapolis Marina, Mears Marina, the Chesapeake Harbour Marina, the Annapolis Landing Marina, and Bert Jabin's Easport. This is also a major location for all conceivable boat repairs and maintenance, and there are yacht brokers located in the marinas, or nearby. Most of these are large marinas and have a full complement of modern facilities including: restaurants, ship's stores, groceries, pump out stations, service technicians for engine repair, electronics sales and service, and sailmakers.

If you have transportation, it is a short trip to Annapolis where you can spend a day or two wandering around the old city, going to the theatre, the movies, visiting the museums, and generally seeing the sights. If you are boat bound, there are plenty of shops and stores within walking distance to occupy your time, and there are grocery markets in the neighborhood.

For all intents and purposes, Eastport is practically a part of Annapolis as it refers to the area between Back and Spa Creeks.

Annapolis is often considered as " the Boating Capital of the World." Consequently, the city's harbor is often extremely congested at certain times of the year and finding a slip or a mooring can be exceptionally difficult. Although they can be congested in their own rights, Eastport and Back Creek do offer you an alternative. It is close enough to Annapolis, with its historic district; St. John's College, the Naval Academy, and the many attractions, restaurants, shops, and grocery stores that it is not a hardship to find your way into the city for a day.

## NAVIGATION

As is Annapolis Harbor and Spa Creek, Back Creek is easily found by simply following the well-marked channel markers, which you pick up while heading into the Severn River. There is shoaling in this area and you should have a chart on hand if you are unfamiliar with these waters. Anchoring in Back Creek is not recommended. Spa Creek has limiting anchoring and there are moorings available through the Annapolis City Dock operation. There are two other anchoring options, the Naval Anchorage and South Anchorage, however, they are somewhat exposed.

*A forest of masts in Eastport.*

# SOUTH RIVER, MD

Selby Bay Yacht Basin

Holiday Point Marina

Long Point

SOUTH RIVER

Shoals

SELBY BAY

South River Marina

Anchor Yacht Basin

Selby Bay Y.C.

Turkey Point Island

Turkey Point Marina

N

NOT TO BE USED FOR NAVIGATION.
Use as a reference only. Consult
recommended charts for navigation.

The South River has a distinct advantage over many anchorages and ports of call because of its close proximity to major cities including Annapolis and Baltimore. It is certainly within a short day's cruise from either city and therefore, makes it a logical stopover.

## NAVIGATION

For the average cruiser, the entrance to the South River is marked by one of the most recognizable navigational aides on the Bay; the Thomas Point Light. Once you have reached it, the channel heading west into the river is easy to follow and the mouth of the river is almost a mile wide giving the mariner plenty of leeway.

Once into the river, the first bay to port is Selby Bay. Although small, it has one of the better anchorages of the area. At first glance, it may be confusing to enter, but with a review of your charts it is not difficult. There are shoals surrounding Long Point and extending from Selby Beach clearly shown on charts.

Beyond Selby Bay are several smaller creeks, most offering outstanding anchorages. Among them are Harness Creek, Aberdeen Creek, and Church Creek. All of these are distinctive in their own rights and choosing one over another for anchoring is dependent upon your desires.

While cruising the South River, you are likely to find yourself in the company of "go fast" boats so keep alert. Speed and noise restrictions have been put into play, and this has helped to make South River much more enjoyable for those mariners utilizing the anchorages or cruising the river.

## ASHORE

Although there are numerous spots to anchor, the South River also has its fair share of marinas. In Selby Bay, there is the Holiday Point Marina, the Selby Bay Yacht Basin, the Turkey Point Marina, the South River Marina and the Anchor Yacht Basin. The area is also the home of the Selby Bay Yacht Club. Further up the river are several marinas including the Liberty Yacht Club and Marina, the Little Island Marina, the Londontowne Marina, the Oak Grove Marina and the Pier 7 Marina.

With the large number of boats on South River, there are the accompanying good number of ship's stores, restaurants and shops. Nearby Route 2 offers malls and grocery stores, and there is little that cannot be found by the visiting boater.

The river and its anchorages are relatively quiet, especially during weekdays. During weekends and holidays, however, you can expect it to be crowded with boats of all sizes and styles. Nearby Annapolis, with its countless shops, restaurants, sights and many activities, is a definite contrast to the relaxing solitude that can be found on South River.

*Mallards on the South River.*

# WEST RIVER, MD

NOT TO BE USED FOR NAVIGATION — Use as a reference only. Consult recommended charts for navigation.

Hartage Yacht Yard

Steamboat Landing Restaurant

Topside Inn & Restaurant

West River Yacht Harbour

WEST RIVER

Pirate's Cove Marina

Chesapeake Yacht Club

N

and south. During the sailing season, however, the local sailors race throughout the length of the river especially around Pirate's Cove Marine. When anchoring near here, you may want to leave plenty of room between yourself and your neighbors to allow for plenty of racing room for these craft.

Another anchoring option, which should be considered, is a few hundred yards beyond the Hartge Yacht Yard where Lerch Creek enters the river. Just off of the Chesapeake Yacht Club is another choice for anchoring although the ground is comprised of more sand than mud. If you choose this site, keep an eye out for pilings, which are visible during the daylight hours but are hard to see at night.

## ASHORE

For those of you who do not want to deal with setting up an anchor, the West River Yacht Harbour, Inc. has slips available for an overnight stay. Both yards mentioned on Parrish Creek also have slips available.

Anyone visiting the West River will find plenty of things to occupy the time. Steamboat Landing Restaurant offers fine cuisine and lodgings for the night and within easy walking distance are a number of small grocery stores and antique shops. Galesville has managed to enter the 21st century with much of its architecture and culture intact and is well worth an evening stroll. Galesville proper also has its full complement of restaurants, which are well known for their food and music.

*A colorful Skipjack bow pulpit.*

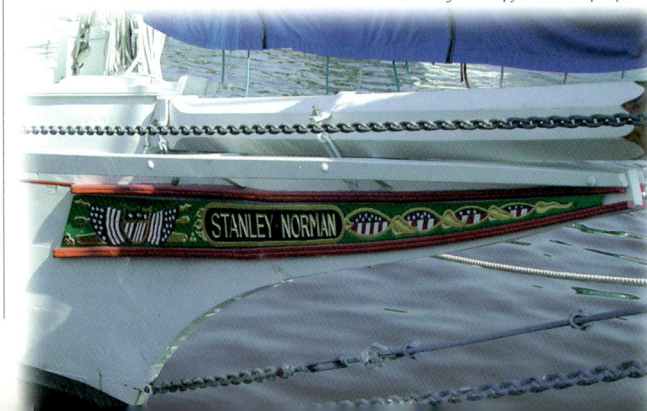

If you are searching for quiet anchorages with enough of the many amenities of the more metropolitan Bay destinations, the West River should be close to the top of your list. West River is able to combine the most positive characteristics of larger ports of call with enough marinas, restaurants, and shops to make it a definite stop.

The West River area has a principal advantage; it is only nine miles from the Chesapeake Bay Bridge, and less than that from major boating havens, such as Annapolis or large marina complexes to the south. For those of you who have difficulty getting away for any amount of time, West River is well within the time frame you face if sailing, and easily within reach in the case of operating a powerboat.

## NAVIGATION

As with a majority of sites outlined in this book, the West River entrance is extremely simple to find and easy to navigate as it is well marked.

Anchoring along the West River is open to the imagination as there is deep water, and several protected coves and creeks, to consider along the river's entire length. Directly opposite Rhode River is Parrish Creek. Although primarily a home for local watermen, it does have several boatyards along its banks including Backyard Boats, and the Parrish Creek Marina / Boat Yard.

The area across from Pirate's Cove Marina, although there are moorings available, is a prime location for dropping the hook as it is well-protected from the north

# ROCKHOLD & TRACEY'S CREEKS

Skipper's Pier Restaurant
Paradise Marina
Shipwright Harbor Marina
Rockhold Creek Marina
ROCKHOLD CREEK
Herrington Harbour North
Calypso Bay
West Marine
TRACEY'S CREEK
Happy Harbor Restaurant
Harbor Cove Marina
Gates Marina

NOT TO BE USED FOR NAVIGATION
Use as a reference only. Consult recommended charts for navigation.

and diesel repairs, fiberglass construction and repairs, painting and polishing, prop service, rigging and spars and electrical/electronics service and sales. A West Marine is on the premises, as well as the Calypso Bay Restaurant and Dock Bar. Adjoining the yard is a fine marina with exceptional amenities. On the shores of Rockhold Creek, there are several other choices in marinas, most of which offer haulouts, mechanical repairs and other services. They include Gates Marina, Shipwright Harbor Marina, Paradise Marina, Harbour Cove Marina and Rockhold Creek Marina.

The Deale Water Taxi, which you can hail on VHF 68, will transport you throughout the area, including to the waterfront restaurants. Among your choices are the Happy Harbour, Skipper's Pier and Fisher's Wharf. The specialities are seafood and some offer live entertainment.

For provisioning, you will require ground transportation to the local 7-Eleven or the Deale IGA, however, a ride should be easy to arrange at any of the marinas. There are several interesting antique shops and other stores in this community, but here the emphasis on boating and fishing.

The widest possible range of marine services and supplies, in addition to outstanding marina facilities, makes the Deale area a favorite for both resident and cruising boaters. This small community offers several restaurants, a large charter fishing fleet, unique shops and stores for provisioning. All are easily reached from nearby marinas.

Lying in the northern stretches of Herring Bay, the activities and marina facilities are centered around the shores of Tracey's Creek and Rockhold Creek.

## NAVIGATION

It is widely accepted Herring Bay itself is a poor choice for an anchoring. It is shallow and exposed from all directions. Your wisest option is to take a slip in one of the marinas along the creek banks.

Both Rockhold Creek and Tracey's Creek are well-marked and easily navigated with adequate depth for deeper draft craft. The recommended approach is from the south, avoiding Long Bar, which is best left to those with local knowledge.

## ASHORE

One of the Bay's largest and most comprehensive yacht yards and marinas, Herrington Harbour North, is situated on the southern shores of Tracey's Creek. This one-stop yard provides the boater with every conceivable service, including on site canvas/sail repair, carpentry, mechanical

*Dockage in a park like setting at Herrington Harbour North on Tracey's Creek.*

Photo Tom Henschel

# HERRINGTON HARBOUR SOUTH, MD

HERRINGTON HARBOUR SOUTH MARINA & RESORT

Herrington Harbour Inn

Marina Office

Bayside Market & Deli

ROSE HAVEN

N

NOT TO BE USED FOR NAVIGATION
Use as a reference only. Consult
recommended charts for navigation.

going on throughout the boating season. Visit the marina's web site at www.herringtonharbour.com for a posting of events and happenings.

Amenities at this port of call are extensive. They include a sauna and fitness center, swimming pools and a private beach, boat and bike rentals, fishing charters, tennis, volleyball, shuffleboard, playgrounds, picnic areas with grills, a gift shop, catering for parties, restaurants, lounges and bars.

Adjacent to the marina offices are stores, the La Mer Beauty Shop and the Bayside Market & Deli, and a courtesy car is available for other shoreside transportation if you need to travel further afield.

For accommodations ashore, the Herrington Harbour Inn offers "Caribbean-style" units on the beach with private patios and hot tubs.

Gas, diesel and repairs are available here. However, haulouts and more extensive marine service are found at Herrington Harbour North, a short distance away.

For boaters seeking seasonal slips, Herrington Harbour South is an excellent choice because of its location for day cruising to many other Bay destinations. Annapolis, St. Michaels, Oxford, Baltimore, Chestertown, and many secluded anchorages are nearby. For the visiting cruiser, the marina is the perfect stopover with its mid-bay location and ease of navigation while transiting the Chesapeake.

Known as the "Caribbean on the Chesapeake Bay", Herrington Harbour South is recognized as one of the region's premiere marina resorts. This facility is actually much like a community onto itself. With hundreds of slips that are occupied by sailboat and powerboat enthusiasts alike, the marina and resort has everything any vacationing boater could desire.

Located at Rose Haven on the Bay, Herrington Harbour South is surrounded by a quiet and very appealing, rural area of the mid-bay on the Western Shore.

## NAVIGATION

Immediate access to the Bay is one of the considerations which accounts for this marina's popularity. Situated at the southern end of Herring Bay, a straightforward channel leads directly into the marina. The channel is readily picked up from the Bay and represents no navigational challenges.

## ASHORE

Reserve your dreams of trekking from shop-to-shop for other Bay destinations, but don't ever expect to be bored at Herrington Harbour South. The boaters within this unique facility are an extremely social group, and there are almost continuous activities

Herrington Harbour South is billed as the "Caribbean on the Chesapeake Bay".

Photo Tom Henschel

# CHESAPEAKE BEACH, MD

**CHESAPEAKE BEACH**

Fishing Creek

Abner's Marina & Boatyard

Fishing Creek Landings Marina

Chesapeake Beach Water Park

Chesapeake Beach Railway Musuem

Rod 'Reel Restaurant

Rod 'N Reel Charter Fishing & Tackle

Windward Key

Well Marked Channel

NOT TO BE USED FOR NAVIGATION
Use as a reference only. Consult
recommended charts for navigation.

It all began with a dream. Chesapeake Beach was to be a haven for the rich living in Washington, D. C. and Baltimore who wanted and needed an escape to the shore during the hot summer months. There was the dream of a railway system connecting these two cities with a destination on the Bay. The railway became more then a dream when it was completed in the late 1890's but for the investors, the dream became a nightmare. Operating a railway system was extremely expensive and over the years, it changed hands several times. The Great Depression and the advent of the automobile also seriously taxed the railroad's operation. Investors tried to buck the downward trend by developing a resort area with roller coasters, a boardwalk for evening strolls, high wire acts, dancing bears,

ballrooms, and an elegant motel called the Belvedere Hotel. The attempts to revitalize the town were to no avail and the dreams of the original investors and those who followed fell by the wayside.

However, Chesapeake Beach did not die with those dreams. Today, even without the amusements dreamed of in the early 20th century, the town has become a Mecca for fishermen and is the home to one of the largest charter fishing fleets on the Bay.

## NAVIGATION

The entrance to Chesapeake Beach is located approximately two miles south of Holland Point and is marked by two large jetties. Tides and currents are constantly changing the depths on the approaches to this harbor and today, the reported depth of the channel is 4.5 feet. Once inside the breakwater and in the creek proper depths, are greater. As this is the homeport for many fishermen and charter fleets, the channel is well maintained. If you want to tie up to a dock for the night, dockage is available. Check with Rod 'N Reel, Charter Fishing and Tackle. There are several marinas here, however, due to a bridge with only a 12-foot fixed vertical clearance, only smaller vessels can reach them. These marinas include Abner's Marina and Boatyard and Fishing Creek Landings Marina.

## ASHORE

For those wishing to take a stroll through Chesapeake Beach, a must is a stop at the Chesapeake Beach Railway Museum which covers the history of the railway from its conception until it was abandoned in the mid 1930's. Although the old amusement park is no longer there, it has been replaced by the Chesapeake Beach Water Park. This is a family oriented town and if you are bringing children, there are plenty of activities to keep everyone occupied. Along with the amusements mentioned, there are an ample number of shops, grocery stores and restaurants to keep you occupied.

Photo by Tom Henschel

*The Chesapeake Beach Railroad Museum.*

# SOLOMONS ISLAND, MD

Drum Point · Patuxent River Naval Air Station · Mill Creek · Washburn's Marina · Harbor Island · Town Center Marina · Calvert Marina · Narrows · Zahniser's Marina · Calvert Marine Museum · Hospitality Harbor Marina · Back Creek · Spring Cove Marina · Comfort Inn Beacon Marina · Holiday Inn

NOT TO BE USED FOR NAVIGATION
Use as a reference only. Consult
recommended charts for navigation.

Forty years ago Solomons Island was a small, isolated backwater area relatively unknown except by the local inhabitants, watermen and boat builders. This port of call is located approximately 40 miles away from the better known harbors of St. Michaels, Oxford, and Annapolis. With the construction of Route 301, and the completion of a major bridge connecting the Solomons with Jackson City and cities to the south and north, the area became a recognized haven for weekenders and retirees from major mid-Atlantic cities. Its continued popularity began to extend to the boating community and it is now one of the major hotspots on the Western Shore.

Other than its beautiful location and accessibility, the Solomons is unique as it offers both quiet anchorages and modern, full service facilities, restaurants and shops all within a few miles of each other. Boaters can be at anchor in Mill Creek for a night or two away from boating traffic and be only 15 minutes away from the marinas and town.

## NAVIGATION

From the Bay, the first landmark is a series of large storage tanks. To the north is an atomic power plant. The entrance to Solomons Island and the Patuxent River is a few miles south of these landmarks. Drum Point is well marked and there is ample water in approaching it. Once past Drum Point, you have two options as shoals locally called "the Flats" splits the

channel. You can hug the north shore or stay mid-river. Both channels are well marked Once past "the Flats", the entrance to the inner regions of the Solomons is straightforward.

The Solomons is divided into three fingers which offer good protection in poor weather and are well marked. " The Narrows ", found to the port, is home to the local vessels. To the north is Back Creek where most of the marinas are found. Although Back Creek does have spots to anchor, you might enjoy a quiet night in Mill Creek which is slightly northeast of Back Creek.

### ASHORE

The Solomons offers a full complement of grocery stores, shops, museums, and marine facilities. A walking tour should include the Calvert Marine Museum, the Drum Point Lighthouse, the Wm. B. Tennison and the J. C. Lore Oyster Processing Plant.

Marinas include: Zahniser's Yachting, Center Spring Cove Marina, Hospitality Harbor Marina, Solomons Point Marina, Washburn's Marina, Harbor Island Marina, Town Center Marina, Comfort Inn Beacon Marina, Mill Creek Boating Center, Calvert Marina, and the Harbor at Solomons.

You have a wide choice of marina options at Solomons Island, as well as excellent anchorages. There are many interesting sites to take in on your visit.

Photo Tom Henschel

# URBANNA, VA

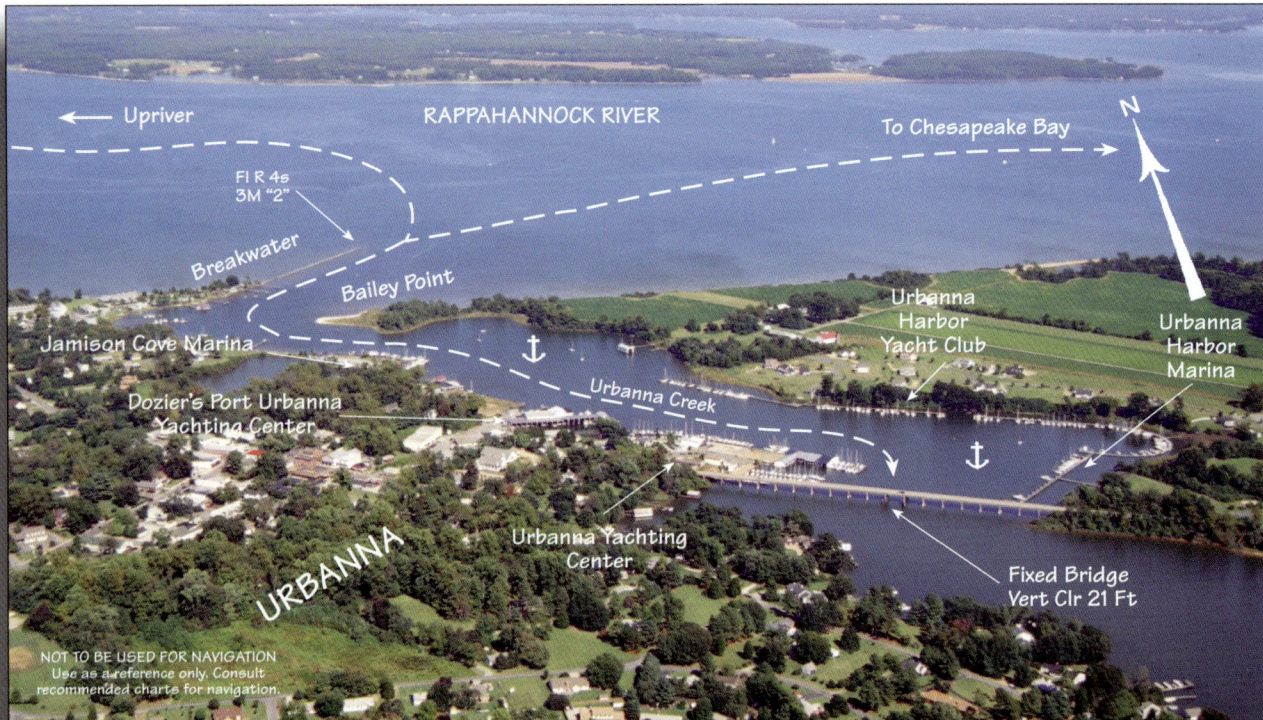

Map labels:
- ← Upriver
- RAPPAHANNOCK RIVER
- To Chesapeake Bay
- N
- Fl R 4s 3M "2"
- Breakwater
- Bailey Point
- Jamison Cove Marina
- Dozier's Port Urbanna Yachting Center
- Urbanna Creek
- Urbanna Harbor Yacht Club
- Urbanna Harbor Marina
- Urbanna Yachting Center
- URBANNA
- Fixed Bridge Vert Clr 21 Ft
- NOT TO BE USED FOR NAVIGATION. Use as a reference only. Consult recommended charts for navigation.

Once a major port for the exportation of tobacco, Urbanna is a quiet and uniquely interesting community with a history dating back more than 300 years. Only several hundred residents call this town home, however, during the first weekend in November, thousands of visitors flock here for the annual Urbanna Oyster Festival.

Parades, an oyster shucking contest, street dances and other events highlight this festival, which was established in the late 1950's. If you are planning on visiting by boat and hope for dockage during this time, call the marinas well in advance.

Situated on the southern shore of the Rappahannock River, Urbanna provides a well-protected harbor that offers a choice of three marinas for transient boaters. All are within easy walking distance to downtown.

## NAVIGATION

Urbanna Creek, approximately 12 miles from the mouth of the Rappahannock River, is the hub for the marinas and service or repair facilities for Urbanna. The creek channel is marked and easily navigated. There are anchoring options within the creek (inside Bailey Point) and also just offshore of the town. A fixed bridge upstream limits traffic to boats with a clearance of less than 21 feet.

## ASHORE

On the creek, there are three marinas that cater to both transient or resident boaters, including the Urbanna Yachting Center, Dozier's Port Urbanna Yachting Center (both offering repairs and service) and the Jamison Cove Marina. The Urbanna Harbor Yacht Club and Urbanna Harbor Marina are private facilities, although the yacht club is open to those with reciprocal agreements from other clubs.

The downtown area sprawls away from Urbanna Creek. The Custom's House, the Tobacco Warehouse, the Old Court House, Fort Nonsense and other sights should be on a first time visitor's plans. There are numerous also fascinating buildings dating from the 18th century throughout the town that make a walking tour worthwhile.

En route, you will also discover a number of antique galleries, gift stores, hardware and marine shops, a grocery store, and other stops that are bound to fill a day of exploration.

Seafood is the main fare at the eateries in Urbanna. These include Shuckers, Beauregards, and Virginia Street Cafe. The Boathouse Cafe overlooks Urbanna Creek, and the same owners operate the Boathouse Bakery. For lighter meals, pizza and other dishes are offered at Colonial Pizza.

With a rich history, and an out-of-the-way flavor, Urbanna is a stop that should be placed upon any cruising agenda.

*A bluefish catch.*

Photo by Tom Henschel

# IRVINGTON, VA

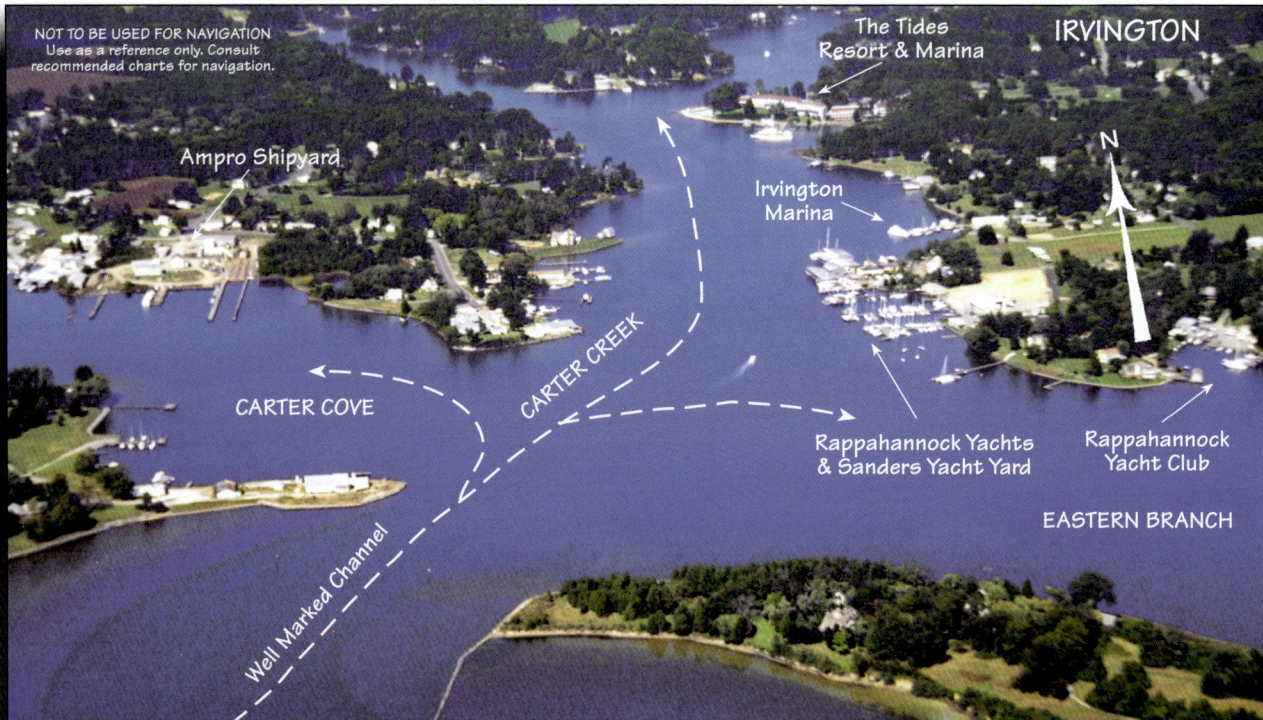

NOT TO BE USED FOR NAVIGATION
Use as a reference only. Consult
recommended charts for navigation.

The Tides
Resort & Marina

IRVINGTON

N

Ampro Shipyard

Irvington
Marina

CARTER CREEK

CARTER COVE

Well Marked Channel

Rappahannock Yachts
& Sanders Yacht Yard

Rappahannock
Yacht Club

EASTERN BRANCH

## NAVIGATION

Entering Carter Creek is easy, as the channel is deep and well marked. If you are searching for a place to anchor, there are several options including Carter Cove, which is immediately to port after entering the creek. If this is your first choice, anchoring is possible beyond the shipyard. Yopps Cove, which is to starboard, has good anchorage and an excellent view of the river and further inland, the Eastern Branch offers some protection from adverse weather.

## ASHORE

The Tides and its marina, which you can easily identify by its unique red roof, is a premiere Bay resort. The Tides offers a fine restaurant and luxurious accommodations in a resort setting. There are several well-established marinas, which also cater to the boating community. In Carter Cove, you will find the Ampro Shipyard. Further up Carter Creek is the Irvington Marina, which offers most of the amenities expected at a large marina.

Rappahannock Yachts and Sanders Yacht Yard also has slips available to transient boats. For those wishing to visit Irvington proper and the immediate area, specifically the old Carter Plantation, The Tides does have vehicles you can rent.

One of the most scenic rivers on the Western Shore is the Rappahannock River, which is south of the Potomac River and north of Norfolk. Its location makes it an easy sail from Solomons Island, the Norfolk area and the Potomac River. If you are searching for another site which has the much needed, quiet atmosphere and solitude that many mariners are searching for, the Rappahannock and towns such as Irvington should be on your list.

As are so many of Virginia's towns, Irvington and its environs are steeped in American history and any history buff interested in learning more about America's past would benefit from a visit. When entering Carter Creek, Carter Cove, found immediately to port, is the commercial center on the creek. At the far end of the cove is the community of Weems, which in its own right, has a long history as having been part of the original Carter Plantation. John Carter, who arrived in 1649 from England, became one of the largest landowners on the Rappahannock. His son, "King" Carter enlarged his father's holdings until at the time of his death, he owned and operated 330,000 acres, 1,000 slaves and possessed 10,000 pounds sterling. Through advantageous marriages, the Carter family continued to expand not only in numbers but also in influence. To date, there are two presidents, several signers of the Declaration of Independence, four governors, and one of the most impressive generals in the Civil War, Robert E. Lee found on the family tree.

*Another view of Irvington .*

# DELTAVILLE, VA

Windmill Point

Chesapeake Cove Marina

Walden Bros. Marina

Dozier's Regatta Point Yachting Center

Stingray Harbor Marina

CHESAPEAKE BAY

Consult Charts For Shoal Water

RAPPAHANNOCK RIVER

Norton's Marina

Norview Marina

Stingray Point

DELTAVILLE

Marked Channel Broad Creek

Deltaville Marina & Andersen Boatworks

Deltaville Yachting Center

Marked Channel Jackson Creek

Stove Point Neck

Ruark's Marina

Fishing Bay Yacht Club

Fishing Bay Harbor Marina

Deagle's Boatyard

FISHING BAY

NOT TO BE USED FOR NAVIGATION
Use as a reference only. Consult recommended charts for navigation.

the Chesapeake because of its protection from all directions except the south.

## ASHORE

Once inside Broad Creek, you have a wide choice of marinas to choose from. Among them are Stingray Harbor Marina, the new Dozier's Regatta Point Yachting Center, Norview Marina, the Deltaville Yachting Center, Chesapeake Cove Marina, Norton's Yacht Sales & Marina and Walden Brothers Marina. There are also several boatyards and repair facilities. On Jackson Creek and Fishing Bay, there is the Deltaville Marina, Ruark Marina, Fishing Bay Harbor Marina and Deagle's Boatyard. The Fishing Bay Yacht Club is also found here.

Walk or bike to nearby downtown Deltaville. There is a number of restaurants including Taylor's, Toby's, the Galley and Sal's Italian Restaurant. Most will provide a ride to and from their establishments. If ice cream or sweets appeal to your palate, visit the Sweet Shoppe, which is also a deli and bakery. For provisioning or supplies, several other shops and grocery stores are scattered throughout the town.

The waters surrounding the Deltaville region are known for excellent fishing, and a number of tournaments are held each year from local marinas. Nearby, other ports of call worthy of a visit, include Urbanna and Irvington, both on the Rappahannock River.

If a laid-back, country setting appeals to you versus more crowded metropolitan areas, Deltaville must rank high on your list of choices for either visiting or permanent dockage. Once a major boat building center for the Chesapeake Bay, recreational boating has become the mainstay of this small community and the town's commerce thrives on its existence.

Nearly a dozen marinas provide outstanding amenities, such as pools, parks, meeting halls and other comforts. Additionally, most provide the widest range of services and repair.

The majority of the marine facilities are centered in the area of Stingray Point and along either Jackson or Broad Creeks.

## NAVIGATION

Broad Creek is entered from the southern shores of the Rappahannock River. The channel leading into the protected basin is well-marked and dredged to accommodate deeper draft sailing vessels which you may find at the surrounding marinas.

The Jackson Creek area is entered from the northern shore of the Piankatank River and a narrow, but plainly marked channel leads into the creek. There is no room for error if you drift outside the channel, since shoals border on both sides.

Jackson Creek and the adjacent Fishing Bay both offer attractive anchoring possibilities. Fishing Bay is a favorite anchorage for many boats transiting

*A closer view of Stingray Point, Broad Creek and its marinas looking east towards Chesapeake Bay and the mouth of the Rappahannock River.*

# HAMPTON, VA

NOT TO BE USED FOR NAVIGATION
Use as a reference only. Consult
recommended charts for navigation.

HAMPTON

Hampton Creek Marina
Bluewater Yachting Center
Sunset Creek
Hampton Y.C.
Va. Air & Space Center
Customs House Marina
Hampton Public Piers
Radisson Hotel
Settlers Landing Road (Fixed Bridge Vert Cl 29')
Joy's Marina
Hampton University
V. A. Hospital
HAMPTON RIVER

Hampton Creek Marina, South Bay Yachting, Bluewater Yachting Center, Sunset Boating Center and the Hampton Roads Marina.

Should you require overnight accommodations, the Radisson Hotel Hampton is located on the waterfront nearby the downtown marinas. The hotel offers fine dining at its Pier-21 restaurant and there is a sports bar on its ground floor. Other eateries are also found on the waterfront and "Restaurant Row" is within walking distance, providing an even greater variety of cuisine choices.

Hampton is rich in history and a tour is a must. Among the sights to include are the Virginia Air and Space Museum, the Hampton History Museum, the NASA Langley Tour, Hampton University, Fort Wool, and the Casement Museum at Fort Monroe.

Hampton University, established to educate freed slaves, is home to the oldest Afro-American museum in the country. Fort Monroe's nickname, " Fort Liberty " speaks for itself as it played a major role in the Civil War. Fort Wool played major roles in the Civil War and both World Wars. It can not be reached by land, but boat tours are available.

With a population of approximately 150,000 people, Hampton offers a good choice of restaurants and shops. With its quaint atmosphere, quiet streets, and more than 350 years of history, Hampton is well worth visiting.

Hampton is another fine choice as a cruising destination, especially if you are looking to avoid the crowds of larger cities. Hampton, founded in 1608, is steeped in American history. Due to its proximity to Union held Fort Monroe, the Confederate Army burned much of the city in 1861. Consequently, many of the earlier houses and buildings do not exist. However, their replacements are worth seeing.

## NAVIGATION

The Hampton River can be approached from the Intracoastal Waterway, the Bay, or the Atlantic Ocean. Refer to your navigation charts for entering the river. Once within the confines of the river, the channel leading to

Hampton is well-marked and easy to navigate. Upstream, is a modern building which houses the Hampton Visitor's Center and directly above the center is a fixed bridge with a vertical clearance of 29 feet.

## ASHORE

If you wish to tie up, slips are available at the Hampton Yacht Club for visitors who are members of reciprocal clubs and at the Hampton Public Pier located between the Visitor's Center and the bridge. For those who want to anchor, there is a spot on the southern side across from the visitor's center and the city docks.

Other marina dockage opportunities abound. These include: the Customs House Marina, Joy's Marina, the

*Downtown Hampton on the waterfront with the Virginia Air and Space Museum in the background.*

Photo Tom Henschel

# NORFOLK & PORTSMOUTH, VA

NORFOLK

To Chesapeake Bay

Tidewater Yacht Marina

Intracoastal Waterway

NOT TO BE USED FOR NAVIGATION
Use as a reference only. Consult recommended charts for navigation.

PORTSMOUTH

other guides and charts for options.

In the wake of 911 and other terrorists acts, it would be remiss not to mention that security is high in the vicinity of the many U.S. Navy ships. Don't be surprised to encounter patrol boats and even snipers aboard berthed vessels. Utilize caution and a no-nonsense approach in your boating operation.

## ASHORE

Among the most popular and largest marinas for transient cruisers are the Tidewater Yacht Marina and the Waterside Marina. The Tidewater Yacht Marina offers 350 slips with a service department and boat lift. Adjoining the Holiday Inn and Renaissance Convention Center, this marina is within walking distance to shops, restaurants (including the on site Armory's Wharf), and local attractions. Across the ICW, the Waterside Marina and Waterside Marketplace offer resort style dockage, shopping and a wide choice of restaurants. Consult local guides for several other area marinas catering to visiting cruisers.

For transportation, choose either a water taxi, or board the Norfolk Trolley, which visits numerous worthwhile sites. There are additionally two museums deserving a stop including Nauticus, the National Maritime Center and the Naval Shipyard Museum.

Norfolk and Portsmouth represent the gateway to the Chesapeake Bay for boats travelling the Intracoastal Waterway north. As these cities are major bases for the U.S. Navy and other shipping, you can expect to encounter all types of vessels ranging from aircraft carriers and destroyers to tugs and barges. The amount of traffic and the huge sizes of many of the ships can be intimidating to the recreational boater.

Nonetheless, with several excellent marinas, a wide variety of restaurants and shopping options, nightlife and many interesting sights, the area is a favorite stopoff point for countless cruisers enroute north or south along the ICW. While industry and the Navy are key to the local economy, you will also find the history of Norfolk and Portsmouth especially interesting. Likewise, there are numerous events throughout the season to keep anyone in the family occupied.

## NAVIGATION

Because of the heavy traffic that you are likely to encounter travelling these waters, it's wise to keep a sharp lookout. Much of the waterway is posted with speed restrictions and to the south, there are numerous bridges with timed openings. You may also encounter various markers that you could be unfamiliar with that are utilized largely by larger ships. Keep a detailed chart handy and you should have little difficulty with navigation. Anchorages are limited and you should consult

*Another view of Portsmouth and Norfolk looking north towards Port Norfolk. Tidewater Yacht Marina is found in the lower left corner and Waterside Marina in the lower right corner.*

# GEORGETOWN, MD

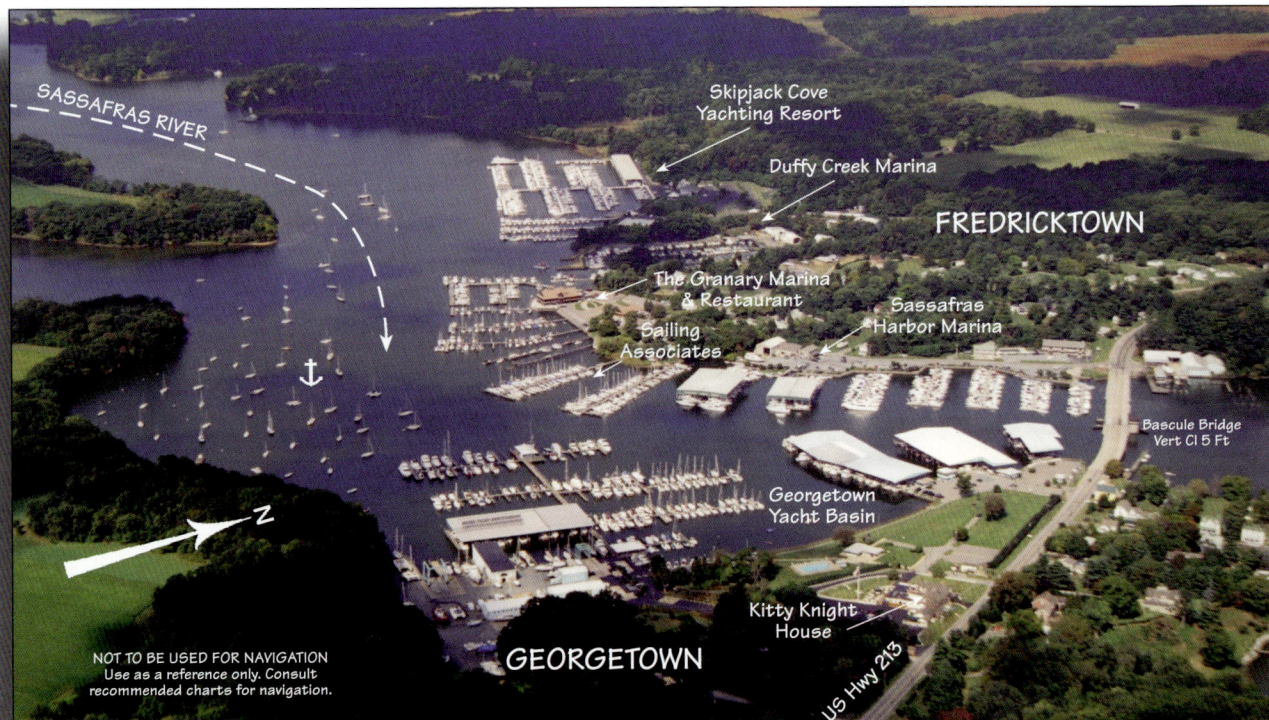

Labels on map:
- SASSAFRAS RIVER
- Skipjack Cove Yachting Resort
- Duffy Creek Marina
- FREDRICKTOWN
- The Granary Marina & Restaurant
- Sassafras Harbor Marina
- Sailing Associates
- Bascule Bridge Vert Cl 5 Ft
- Georgetown Yacht Basin
- Kitty Knight House
- GEORGETOWN
- US Hwy 213
- N

NOT TO BE USED FOR NAVIGATION. Use as a reference only. Consult recommended charts for navigation.

The Sassafras River is unquestionably one of the Chesapeake Bay area's most scenic and impressive inland waterways. Winding its way through high bluffs and grassy knolls, the river is a much favored cruising area for sailors and powerboaters alike. However, because of this river's popularity, you can expect it to be occupied with other boaters on busy weekends. While there are some speed restricted areas, you will find many high speed powerboats and water skiers sharing the Sassafras.

Georgetown, located near the headwaters of the river and at the intersection of U.S. Highway 213, is not truly a town in the strictest sense. There are some shops and homes, but little in the way of provisioning. This area is actually two communities, Georgetown on the north shore and Fredricktown on the south, and these communities were established in the 1700's.

## NAVIGATION

Georgetown is located several miles from the mouth of the river, which is easily navigated in a deep well-marked channel. Near the entrance is the small community of Betterton. This is a popular spot because of its excellent beach, anchorage and limited dockage (free for one night). Travelling up the river there are several peaceful anchorages and tributaries that can be explored by dingy.

The highway bridge has a clearance of only five feet, however, a bridge tender is on duty around the clock. There is ample room for anchoring in the vicinity of the marinas, and moorings are also available.

## ASHORE

Marinas with more than 100 slips are the norm here. These are all modern resort style facilities with pools and comforting amenities. Most are located on the north shore, including the Skipjack Cove Yachting Resort, Duffy Creek Marina, Granary Marina & Restaurant, Sailing Associates and Sassafras Harbor Marina. However, on the southern shore is The Georgetown Yacht Basin.

There are several restaurant choices in this community, with most being located within the marina complexes.

Perched high on a bluff overlooking the river on the northern shore is the Kitty Knight House. This inn and restaurant were built in the 1730's and have a colorful and fascinating history revolving around the War of 1812. Elegant dining is offered inside, as well as service porchside overlooking the river and marinas.

Although Georgetown lacks stores for provisioning, nearby Galena does have a good community market. Galena (about a mile and a half from the bridge) also is known for its antique shops.

The Sassafras River and Georgetown deserves their degree of popularity. With fine anchorages and outstanding marinas, the area is certainly worthy of a visit.

*The small town of Betterton near the mouth of the Sassafras River.*

# FAIRLEE CREEK, MD

FAIRLEE CREEK

Beach

Mears Great
Oak Landing
Marina

NOT TO BE USED FOR NAVIGATION
Use as a reference only. Consult
recommended charts for navigation.

You should refer to charts to check the actual depth along the beach but there appears to be plenty of water. If you are inclined to anchor, across from the Mears Great Oak Landing there is a wide expanse of deep water with good holding ground. It is extremely well protected from winds of all directions. If you wish to tie up to a slip, Great Oak Landing has a number of transient slips available among its 350 slips.

## ASHORE

This is an area that is certainly secluded; (Chestertown, the closest large town, is approximately 12 miles away), and does not have many of the typical tourist attractions found elsewhere. However, the marina facility does have a large restaurant, a conference center, a waterfront bar (Jellyfish Joel's) and an outside crab deck. It would be advisable to make reservations beforehand, especially on weekends. Additionally, the marina complex has a small grocery store for basic supplies, a ship's store, a pool, hot tub, tennis, basketball and volleyball courts, a playground for the kids, a miniature golf course, a nine-hole executive golf course, and lodging. For those of you who really want to get away for a night ashore in an elegant bed and breakfast, the Great Oak Manor, is a stone's throw away.

*A view of Mears Great Oak Landing Marina.*

Fairlee Creek and Mears Great Oak Landing Marina are a few miles north of Tolchester Beach and Rock Hall on the Eastern Shore.

Unlike many of the other sites covered in this book, Fairlee Creek is much smaller and does not have as many facilities found in larger ports. Actually, it is because of its seclusion, its lack of shops, tourist attractions, and amenities which has made it extremely popular among Bay yachtsmen who are looking for a little solitude for a night or two after a busy week in the office. Another plus, obviously, is its close proximity to the larger cities on the Bay including Baltimore and Annapolis. Fairlee Creek is well within a day's sail. Certainly, its close location to the Bay proper is an added bonus.

## NAVIGATION

Entering or leaving Fairlee Creek can create a little excitement for the boater. The entrance is narrow and currents can be strong. Be prepared for this and compensate for any current while entering or leaving the creek. As it is a small entrance, there is also going to be a lot of boating activity especially on weekends. As the mouth is narrow, the more boating activity there is at any given time means that you have to be prepared and on your toes.

Once inside the creek, you have plenty of options to review. Along one side of the creek is a beautiful beach where boats can actually anchor, stern or bow to the beach for picnics or quiet walks on the shore.

Photo by Tom Henschel

# ROCK HALL, MD

Shallow Water Off Swan Point (Consult Charts)

Swan Creek (Observe Seasonal Markers)

Moonlight Bay Inn & Marina

Gratitude Marina

Swan Creek Marina

Osprey Point Marina & Yacht Club

Spring Cove Marina

Kent County Marina

GRATITUDE

The Haven

North Point Marina

P. E. Pruitt's

Haven Harbour Marina

ROCK HALL

Rock Hall Harbor (Shoal In Center)

Rock Hall Marine Railway

Rock Hall Landing Marina

Waterman's Crab House

The Sailing Emporium

NOT TO BE USED FOR NAVIGATION
Use as a reference only. Consult recommended charts for navigation.

provides harbor protection. Travelling north in the channel towards Swan Creek, which leads to Gratitude and the Bay known as "The Haven", you will encounter temporary, seasonal markers after passing the northern point of Gratitude. Reportedly one mistake that numerous boaters have made is attempting to cut across the flats extending west of Swan Point. There is shallow water that is suited only for shallow draft craft.

## ASHORE

Rock Hall boasts more than a dozen marinas and boatyards. Among those catering to transients or vacation oriented boaters are Haven Harbour Marina, Osprey Point Marina & Yacht Club, Swan Creek Marina, the Sailing Emporium, Moonlight Bay Inn & Marina, Gratitude Marina, Spring Cove Marina and North Point Marina & Motel. The character and size of these marinas varies widely and most offer yacht sales and repairs.

There are also a number of restaurants that provide dockage for visiting boaters including P.E. Pruitt's, Waterman's Crab House Restaurant and the Dockside Cafe. A visit downtown with its other restaurants and shops is a must, as is a stop at the nearby Waterman's Museum.

O n first impressions, Rock Hall seems to have more boats in marinas than residents. This quiet, small Eastern Shore community is a hub for sailing activity. Part of this is due to its location and quick access to the Chesapeake Bay. Superb marinas, a town with a true Chesapeake flavor, stores for provisioning and a variety of restaurants are other deciding factors for Rock Hall being a foremost Bay destination.

In a bygone era, this town was a major shipping port. Industry eventually shifted to the harvesting of seafood and ultimately towards recreational boating. It still is an excellent area for fishing, and a good number of boats are available for charter. However, the principal activity focuses around sailing.

## NAVIGATION

Rock Hall is not an area to "wing it" in regards to navigation, especially if you are unfamiliar with the waters. Groundings are not that uncommon for those unfamiliar with the waters. However, if you consult your charts carefully, you will have no problems negotiating the channels leading into the harbor and neighboring marinas. When in doubt, contact any of the marine establishments via VHF. They will be pleased to offer you advice.

Here are just a few notes to keep in mind. When entering Rock Hall Harbor, the channel actually circles shoals in the center. Markers surround this shoal area, with marinas and other establishments with dockage bordering the harbor. A breakwater at the entrance

*Downtown Rock Hall*

Photo by Tom Henschel

# CHESTERTOWN, MD

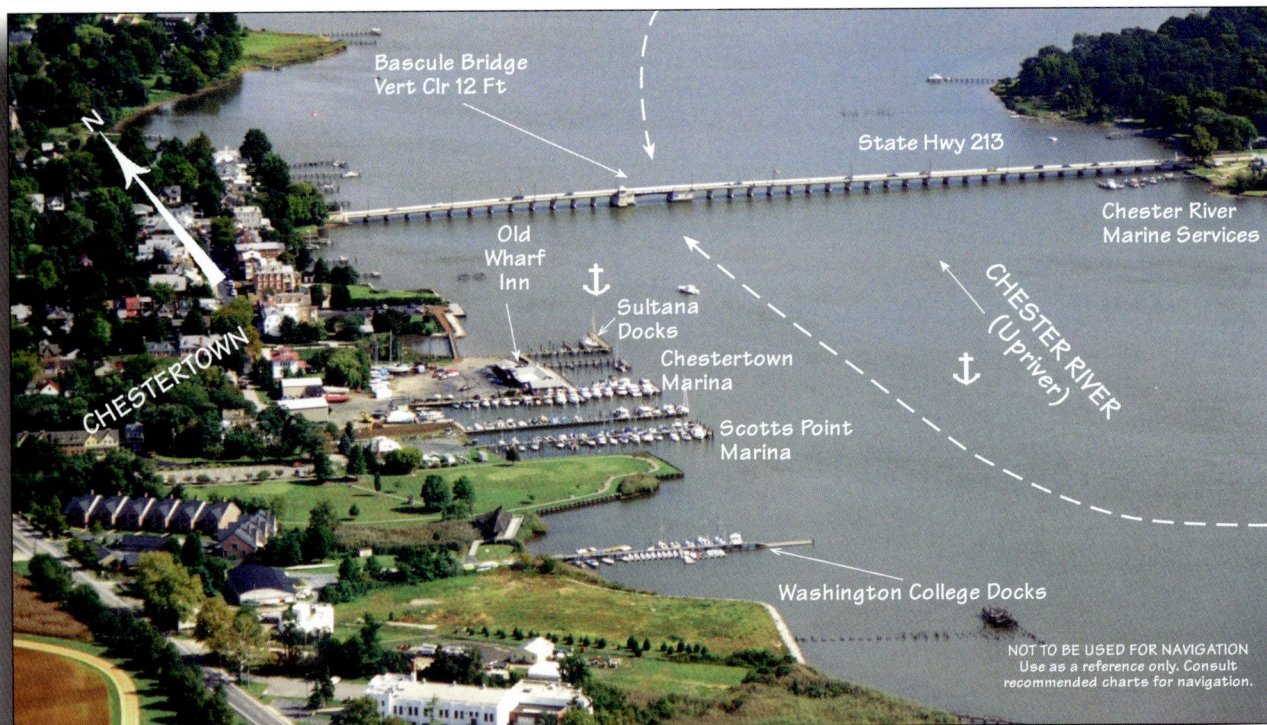

Map labels:
- Bascule Bridge Vert Clr 12 Ft
- State Hwy 213
- Chester River Marine Services
- Old Wharf Inn
- Sultana Docks
- Chestertown Marina
- Scotts Point Marina
- CHESTER RIVER (Upriver)
- CHESTERTOWN
- N
- Washington College Docks
- NOT TO BE USED FOR NAVIGATION Use as a reference only. Consult recommended charts for navigation.

**H**istoric Chestertown, situated on the upper reaches of the Chester River, is one of the finest reflections of a bygone Colonial era. Many of the town's buildings and homes have been restored and a walking tour of Chestertown is truly a step back into time.

Chestertown is, in fact, one of Maryland's oldest communities. It was an important shipping and trade center for many years. Today it is a quiet and an unusually attractive community that has managed to preserve its heritage and remarkable character. It is also immensely appealing to visiting boaters.

## NAVIGATION

Located approximately 20 miles from the mouth of the Chester River near Kent Island Narrows, Chestertown is reached through a deep and well-marked river channel. En route there are several tributaries that provide excellent anchorages, as well as a number of marine facilities. While the river is easily navigated, keep tidal changes in mind when anchoring, as at certain times the current can be substantial.

## ASHORE

There are two principal marinas within walking distance of downtown; the Chestertown Marina and Scotts Point Marina. Both offer transient slips, but on busy summer weekends it is best to call ahead for reservations. The Chestertown Marina has fuel, showers, a ship's store and a repair facility with a haulout lift.

Stop by the nearby Kent County Chamber of Commerce and pick up a walking tour map of the town before setting out. Bicycle rentals are also available close to the marinas.

Activities abound in this charming town. One of the most notable is the Chestertown Tea Party held on Memorial Day weekend. This celebrates an event in 1774 when colonists protested unfair taxes by dumping overboard a cargo of tea from the *Geddes* into the river. The weekend agenda includes a reenactment of the event, a parade, reggatas and parties.

Another worthwhile sight is the Schooner *Sultana*. The schooner is a reproduction of a 1767 vessel that was originally built in Boston. Primarily utilized as a sailing educational classroom, sailing tours are also available to the public. The *Sultana* is docked at the city wharf and offices are located downtown.

A Chestertown visit would not be complete without a tour of Washington College. Established in 1782 with the personal assistance of George Washington, it is the 10th oldest college in the country.

In addition to the many interesting shops, you will find downtown, there are a number of excellent restaurants. The Old Wharf Inn, specializing in local seafood, is located the closest to the marinas. Other Chestertown restaurants include the Imperial Hotel, La Ruota Ristorante, the Black-Eyed Susan, Andy's, Ellen's Family Restaurant, The Feast of Reason, Oconnors Pub, Alexander's, the Blue Heron Cafe and Play It Again Sam coffee shop.

For those desiring a night ashore, Chestertown boasts several fine bed and breakfast style inns, including the White Swan Tavern where you can enjoy a daily afternoon tea.

*The Schooner* Sultana. *A reproduction of a 1767 vessel which once sailed local waters.*

Photo Tom Henschel

# STEVENSVILLE & BAY BRIDGE, MD

To Baltimore & Points North

William P. Lane Jr. Memorial Bridge

To Annapolis & Points South

Marked Channel

CHESAPEAKE BAY

Chesapeake Bay Beach Club

Hemingway's Restaurant & Lola's

Bay BridgeMarina & North Atlantic Marine Group

Bay Bridge Airport

N

NOT TO BE USED FOR NAVIGATION
Use as a reference only. Consult recommended charts for navigation.

## ASHORE

The Bay Bridge Marina offers a variety of services to the travelling boater including a dockside cafe, Hemingway's Restaurant and Lola's Tropical Bar, a pool, a hot tub, a full service yard, emergency repairs, 310 slips including spots for transients, a shop for marine supplies, an extremely large, 16,000 square-foot service facility, VCR movie rentals, a yacht broker, and a fantastic view of the Bay.

Because of its close proximity to Stevensville and Kent Island, you can travel beyond the marina proper. to visit and enjoy the amenities of the surrounding communities. If you need provisions, several large chain grocery stores are located across the main highways. Near the marina, is the Kent Island Depot, which specializes in gourmet quality foods and has a good selection of wines and beer.

Adjacent to the Marina is the Chesapeake Beach Club, which is available to mariners, and has a variety of canoes and kayaks for rent. If you are a pilot, there is the thriving Bay Bridge Airport, which is instrument rated.

Stevensville offers the transient mariner a variety of shops and restaurants, and there are several antique shops which should not be missed if you are into collecting treasures from bygone eras.

During the last weekend in April, the Bay Bridge Marina hosts the Chesapeake Bay Yacht Expo which has become a major Bay boating event.

Connecting the two sides of the Bay from Kent Island and the outskirts of Annapolis is one of the two landmark bridges traversing the Bay. The William P. Lane Jr. Memorial Bridge (more commonly known as the Bay Bridge), which celebrated its first 50 years in the summer of 2002, it is one of the longest bridges in the world. With a vertical clearance of 186 feet, it can be seen and used as a reference point for all boaters from both the northern and southern reaches of the Bay. In fact, this landmark is used as the dividing line and reference point between the various regions of the Bay in many of the waterway guides used today.

Because of its visibility, its location, and the presence of deep water, the land surrounding the bridge, especially on the Eastern Shore, is home to several marinas which have a full complement of boating facilities, shops, grocery stores, and amenities.

## NAVIGATION

As is much of the Bay, the channel leading under the Bay Bridge is well marked and easy to follow. For those who find themselves looking for a spot to tie up due to a change in the weather, a lack of wind, or a desire to partake in the many amenities in Stevensville and Kent Island, a well-marked channel leads into the Bay Bridge Marina. This marina is located just south of the bridge on the Eastern Shore.

*Castle Harbor Marina is a major marina complex just north of the Bay Bridge.*

# KENT ISLAND NARROWS, MD

Castle Harbor Marina

Restaurants & Dockage

Lippincott Marine

Kent Island Yacht Club

Mears Point Marina Complex

Harris Crab House

Red Eye's

Fixed Bridge Hwy 50/301 Vert Cl 65 Ft

Annie's

Piney Narrows Yacht Haven

KENT ISLAND NARROWS

NOT TO BE USED FOR NAVIGATION
Use as a reference only. Consult recommended charts for navigation.

## ASHORE

As mentioned, the Narrows is home to some major marina complexes. Mears Point Marina is a large marina complete with its own state-of-the art fitness center. On the premises is the Red Eye's Dock Bar where you will always find a lively crowd and entertainment on weekends. Lippincott Marine is another large marina facility with approximately 200 slips. This is a family oriented marina featuring a pool, bathhouses, laundry and a marine store. Lippincott is a full-service facility with haulout and repairs. Piney Narrows Yacht Haven is another fine marina facility that offers condominium slips for sale.

One of the favorite reasons for visiting the Narrows is the variety of dining. Among the several restaurants are the Harris Crab House, Fishermen's Village with two dining establishments and a seafood market, the Jetty Restaurant, Angler's Restaurant and Marina, the Crab Deck and Annie's Paramount Steak House. Most offer dockage and the atmosphere ranges from casual to upscale. Pedestrian paths make it easy for visitors to walk from the marinas to any restaurant.

Other stops worthy of a visit include the Queen Anne County Visitor Center and the Chesapeake Exploration Center.

Golfers may want to visit the nearby Queenstown Harbor Golf Links, which was named the best public golf course in the state.

*A crab feast at Harris Crab House.*

While representing a useful shortcut from the northeastern Bay to points south, the Kent Island Narrows has, in recent years, developed into a major boating center, especially during weekends.

In times past, the Narrows was largely occupied by seafood and fish processing plants. Although some remain, today, the industry is mainly devoted to tourism, dining and boating.

With several major marinas all within the vicinity of the Narrows, you can expect weekends to be bustling throughout this area.

## NAVIGATION

Although travelling through the Kent Island Narrows will save you several miles versus rounding the island, a drawbridge with a vertical clearance of 18 feet may slow your progress. From May through October this bridge opens on the half hour from 6 a.m. to 9 p.m. However, at times you can expect heavy traffic transiting the bridge, requiring a sharp eye. Currents can also be a factor through the narrow bridge fenders.

Regardless of which direction you are approaching the Narrows, follow the channel carefully. Consult your charts and other guides. This winding channel can be somewhat tricky to navigate, especially with draft limitations, and then there is little room for error. Note that the red and green navigation aides reverse themselves after passing through the bridge.

Photo Tom Henschel

# ST. MICHAELS, MD

Inn At Perry Cabin

Crab Claw Restaurant

Chesapeake Bay Maritime Museum

Higgins Yacht Yard

Marked Channel

St. Michaels Harbour Inn & Marina

St. Michaels Marina

Town Dock Restaurant

St. Michaels Crab House & Bar

ST. MICHAELS

NOT TO BE USED FOR NAVIGATION
Use as a reference only. Consult recommended charts for navigation

St. Michaels reigns as among one of the most popular cruising destinations on Chesapeake Bay. This community relies almost solely on tourism, and thousands of visitors flock here throughout the warmer seasons.

While other towns may not handle this influx of tourists well, St. Michaels' business owners deserve credit as they have perserved the charm and sophistication of their town's character.

Like most other Eastern Shore communities, history plays an important role in its heritage. St. Michaels name was taken from an Episcopal parish that was established in 1677. Shipbuilding was once an important industry, and the famed "Baltimore Clippers" were constructed here.

## NAVIGATION

The Miles River leads to St. Michaels and the channel is well-marked. However, follow the channel closely as there are areas of shoaling. Once off the town, entrance markers are picked up that will lead you into the harbor. There are several good anchorage areas to choose from and the town provides dingy docks.

## ASHORE

There are three marinas to choose from, including the St. Michaels Marina (formerly the St. Michaels Town Dock Marina), St. Michaels Harbour Inn & Marina and Higgins Yacht Yard. All are within easy walking distance to the downtown area. The Harbour Inn & Marina

provides hotel accommodations, fine dining, and a swimming pool. The St. Michaels Marina also has a pool, as well as three restaurants on the premises and very competitive fuel prices. It's is best to call ahead for reservations at any of these busy marinas.

Restaurants abound in this small community and the fare ranges from burgers to romantic, gourmet meals. There are also a number of excellent crab and seafood establishments. A water taxi is available for transporting visitors around the harbor or tours. Horse drawn carriages are another option.

Talbot Street is the main thoroughfare and here you will find a wide spectrum of shopping possibilities. The shops and their offerings are tasteful and unique. Numerous historical sights dating back into the 1700 -1800's are another feature of this community.

Another attraction is the Chesapeake Bay Maritime Museum, located on the waterfront. The museum, in nine exhibit buildings, houses the world's largest collection of traditional Chesapeake Bay boats and the 1870's Hooper Strait Lighthouse. Many annual events and festivals revolve around the museum.

Choices in accommodations are extensive, ranging from bed and breakfast inns to luxury hotels, and for the golf enthusiast, an outstanding 18-hole golf course is nearby.

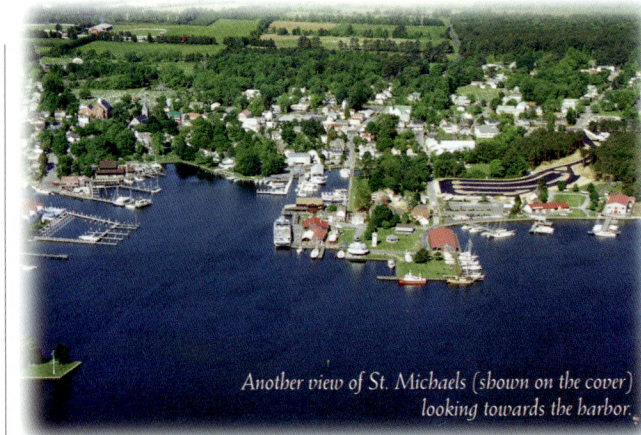

*Another view of St. Michaels (shown on the cover) looking towards the harbor.*

# KNAPPS NARROWS, MD

are likely to be in the company of other boaters transiting the Narrows. Also, be aware that the current can be a factor as you wait on a bridge opening.

It is interesting to note that while this bridge is just a few years old, it was engineered and built to replicate the old bridge as closely as possible. The old bridge was dismantled and then reassembled as an exhibit at the Chesapeake Bay Maritime Museum in St. Michaels.

## ASHORE

In the Narrows itself, marinas include the Knapps Narrows Marina, Tilghman Island Marina, Tilghman Island Inn and Severn Marina Services. On the Choptank side, just to the south, you will find dockage at Harrison's Country Inn and Tilghman-On-The-Chesapeake. All have transient dockage and some have amenities including accommodations and swimming pools.

Treat yourself to true Chesapeake-style dining on Tilghman Island. Seafood is served at its best at several area establishments including the Bridge Restaurant, Bay Hundred Restaurant, the Tilghman Island Inn, and Harrison's Chesapeake House.

The nearby Island Market and the Tilghman Country Store can provide you with provisions and are only a short walk from the marinas.

Knapps Narrows has become increasingly popular with boaters because of its relaxed atmosphere, a few excellent marine facilities and several options for great food.

The Narrows, at Tilghman Island, has a long history as a waterman's center, and that heritage is still apparent today. There is a large fleet of working boats here, as well as a small sportfishing charter boat fleet. During most days, you will find the Narrows area extremely quiet and peaceful. However, weekends are likely to bring crowds of boaters through the waterway and to the surrounding docks with their outdoor bars, decks and dining rooms. The Knapps Narrows is also the site for several festival-style events throughout the season.

## NAVIGATION

Part of Knapps Narrows popularity as a destination is due to it being a significant shortcut from the Bay into the Choptank River. Should you be cruising from the northern section of the Bay to St. Michaels, Oxford or the Choptank, the Narrows will save you several miles. The channels on either the Bay side or from the Choptank are well marked and the entrances are easily spotted. Consult your charts. However, as reported these channels are prone to shoaling, and it is recommended that you follow navigational aides closely.

Also note that at either entrance, the rule of red right returning applies.

During busy times, when you approach the bridge, you

The "new" Knapps Narrows bridge at Tilghman Island.

# OXFORD, MD

Campbell's Town
Creek Boatyard

Bates Marine
Basin

Bachelor
Point

Campbell's Bachelor
Point Yacht Co.

Crockett Bros.
Boatyard

Pier Street Marina

Town Creek

Tred Avon
Yacht Club

TRED AVON
RIVER

Schooner's
Landing

OXFORD

Cutts & Case

Oxford Boat
Yard

Ferry
Wharf

Mears Yacht
Haven

NOT TO BE USED FOR NAVIGATION
Use as a reference only. Consult
recommended charts for navigation.

Oxford is an Eastern Shore community that seems to be created by the genius of Disney. This is a picture perfect village with well-kept houses reminiscent of Cape Cod. Well cared for flower gardens surround these residences and there is an obvious pride by the owners in their property. Sunday mornings you will find friendly residents strolling in tow with their dogs from their homes to the local store for the newspaper. The atmosphere is relaxed and friendly.

In the late 1600's this well protected harbor was once a port of entry and a major shipping center. Later in time the harvest of oysters became its major industry. Oxford's lengthy history and strong bonds with the water remain evident today. Business in the town revolves around boating and its related industries.

## NAVIGATION

Situated on the eastern shore of the Tred Avon River, fairly deep waters practically surround Oxford. Any trouble spots are clearly marked. The river itself is outstanding for sailing. In fair weather a favorite anchorage (called the Strand) is located just off the town beach. Here you will often find a large number of boats anchored near the beach which is accessible by dinghy.

A well-marked channel leads into Town Creek where you will find marinas, restaurants and several repair facilities. There are additional anchoring options inside the mouth of the creek.

## ASHORE

There are a number of fine marinas found within Town Creek, and your choices may depend on requirements. Some lean towards a resort atmosphere, while others combine a marina and boatyard. Mears Yacht Haven is the first you will find to starboard upon entering the creek. This marina has transient slips available and features a ship's store, fuel and a pool. Nearby is the Oxford Boatyard and Crockett Brothers Boatyard. Both provide slips and also repairs and maintenance. Others in Town Creek include Cutts & Case, Schooner's Landing (with restaurants, bars and dockage), Campbell's Town Creek Boatyard, the Oxford Yacht Agency and Bate's Marine. On the opposite side of Oxford, along the Tred Avon River, are two other marinas, Pier Street and Campbell's Bachelor Point Yacht Company. Oxford is also the home of the Tred Avon Yacht Club and the club is located adjacent to the Oxford-Bellevue Ferry, one the nation's longest running ferry services.

Among your restaurant choices are Latitude 38° Bistro & Spirts (which will provide transportation for visiting boaters), the Pier Street Restaurant, the Mill Street Grille, the Robert Morris Inn and Mathilda's. For provisions, you can also stock up on groceries, beer and wine at the Oxford Market. There are several craft and antique shops including, the Oxford Mews, which is a unique, old fashioned emporium.

Sights worth taking in include a downtown museum and a reproduction of the old customs house. The town can be walked easily within a few hours, and bicycles are also available for rent. For those wishing a night ashore, overnight accommodations are found in several bed and breakfast inns.

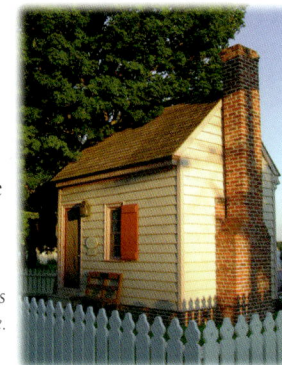

*A reproduction of the colonial times Oxford customs house.*

Photo by Tom Henschel

# CAMBRIDGE, MD

CAMBRIDGE

To Cambridge Creek

Cambridge Municpal
Yacht Basin

Cambridge
Yacht Club

US Hwy 50

Choptank River

Fixed Bridge
Vert Cl 50 Ft

NOT TO BE USED FOR NAVIGATION
Use as a reference only. Consult
recommended charts for navigation.

head into the creek, or to the Cambridge Municipal Yacht Basin just off to starboard.

## ASHORE

The Cambridge Municipal Yacht Basin is a modern, well-managed facility that offers transient dockage and accompanying amenities. Nearby is the Cambridge Yacht Club which welcomes visitors from reciprocating clubs.

Inside Cambridge Creek, you will find a protected anchorage, and there is a bulkhead (Cambridge Marine Terminal) where you can find overnight transient dockage.

The creek is home to several marine-oriented businesses, some of which may provide dockage. They include Yacht Maintenance, Cambridge Marine Ltd., Generation III Marine and Mid-Shore Electronics. The Gator House Restaurant and Snappers Waterfront Cafe are also nearby. On the other side of the bridge, a new Hyatt Hotel and marina opened in 2002.

Stop by the Dorchester County's Visitor Center at Sailwinds Park, directly on the river, and pick up brochures on walking tours of Cambridge. There are dozens of historic homes and sites in the town that are worthwhile viewing.

*Chesapeake sailing.*

Although Cambridge lacks the glitz and glamour of some of its neighboring tourist-oriented communities, it should rank high as a stopover, especially if you are planning on cruising the Choptank River.

The Choptank River offers a wide range of cruising options with many fine anchorages and excellent sailing. Cambridge is a logical port of call for exploring this interesting river.

Cambridge is one of the oldest communities in Maryland. Since it was settled in 1684, it has boasted an illustrious history and was once known as the "Queen City" of the Eastern Shore.

British trading ships visited Cambridge carrying back a range of goods including tobacco and muskrat pelts.

Lumber then played an important role in this town's progression. Eventually this led to boat building and ultimately Cambridge became a hub for oyster harvesting, packing and shipping.

At one point, everyday hundreds of Skipjacks departed from the town docks to the productive oyster beds. Only two remain in Cambridge today, and they both offer boat tours.

## NAVIGATION

The Choptank River is wide and easily navigated for an approach to Cambridge. Entrance markers for the channel that leads into Cambridge Creek are readily picked up and the channel is deep and well-marked. Your options are to

# TANGIER & SMITH ISLANDS, MD & VA

TANGIER ISLAND

Tangier Airport

Parks Marina

TANGIER

Entrance From Chesapeake Bay

Overhead Power Cable (82 ft.)

NOT TO BE USED FOR NAVIGATION
Use as a reference only. Consult
recommended charts for navigation.

accommodate a boat for the night.

Reaching Tangier Island from Tangier Sound is relatively simple. From the Bay. the channel is well marked, and the depth averages approximately nine feet. Once reaching the harbor, there are transient slips available at Parks Marina. There is only one small basin west of the Parks Marina in which you can anchor.

## ASHORE

Ewell, on Smith Island is the most accessible hamlet of the three. Here there are several points of interest worthy of a visit. For crab cakes, a sandwich, or a few necessary provisions, there is Ruke's Store, and a night's lodging may be found at the Bayside Inn. For the tourists coming in on the tour boats, there is food available at the Bayside Inn which serves a lunch buffet. The tour boats tie up at the docks near the inn. For those interested in culture, the Smith Island Center is well worth a visit and of course, there are some small antique shops where a treasure or two maybe found.

Although smaller in size, Tangier Island offers a few more ammenities than Smith Island. Gas and dockage is available at Parks Marina, as is ice on the piers. Several restaurants are located in the small hamlet including Hilda Crockett's on Main Street, Mrs. Crockett's Chesapeake House, the Fisherman's Corner and the Islander.

For three hundred years, Tangier and Smith Islands were essentially cut off from the Maryland and Virginia mainlands. Originally thought to have been one large island, over time it has become two, separated by five miles of open, shallow water. Consequently, the islanders have strong cultural ties and ties to the Bay and yet, have developed their own unique characters.

Even today, with an increase in boat tours from Crisfield, Reedville, and Onancock and more communication with the mainland, visitors will note a distinctive brogue reminiscent of the Elizabethan era.

## NAVIGATION

Both islands can be reached from Tangier Sound and the Bay. Ewell, on Smith Island, is best approached from the Bay as the channel is well-marked and there are two large jetties at the entrance. The water depth ranges from seven to fourteen feet but it is imperative that you stay between the markers. Approaching Smith from Tangier Sound, you have to navigate through smaller channels etched into the marsh. Although it is well marked, currents can be a concern and care should be taken. Once you have entered the basin in Ewell, it would be advisable to check in your various guides and your charts to confirm water depths as they do vary from year-to-year. There are places to tie up on the piers along the channel, however room has to be made for the tour boats. Available anchorage is limited to only one site, which can

*Smith Island and its communities.*

# CRISFIELD, MD

NOT TO BE USED FOR NAVIGATION
Use as a reference only. Consult
recommended charts for navigation.

Little
Annemessex River

Somers Cove
Marina

Sea
Mark
Marine

CRISFIELD

N

## ASHORE

Somers Cove Marina is a large marine facility with approximately 485 slips. It features a pool and golfers can enjoy their pasttime at a course close by. The marina is also convieniently located near the downtown area.

Sea Mark Marine, which is located to starboard and north of the harbor, provides slips for transients.

Adjacent to the marina is the Crisfield Heritage Foundation and Museum. For local information, the chamber of commerce office is a short walk away.

You will never find fresher crabs than in Crisfield and dining options where they are served include the Waterman's Inn, Captain's Galley, Side Street Seafood Market & Restaurant and Peppy's Pub. For those wishing to eat aboard, provisions are available at the downtown Meatland.

Just six miles away, pay a visit to Smith Island and Tangier Islands. These islands are home to seperate unique communities including Ewell, Tylerton and Rhodes Point. There is a marina which provides over-night dockage on Tangier Island, and there are limited anchoring options. Transportation on these islands is limited and your choice of getting around is either by foot, a golf cart, or a bicycle. The friendly residents of these villages are largely watermen working the crab industry. There is a handful of restaurants on each island that serve up local seafood fare.

While somewhat off the beaten path, the Crisfield area offers a great number of interesting sights, and provides a true glimpse into a disappearing Chesapeake Bay way of life.

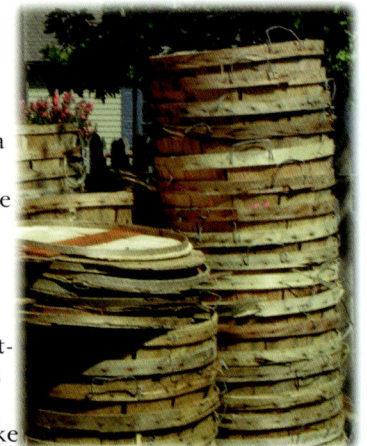

Crab baskets waiting to be filled.

Crisfield ranks as one of the most convenient stopover destinations for cruisers who are travelling north or south along the Intracoastal Waterway.

As it was once a center for commercial oystering on the Chesapeake, a railway extended the length of the Eastern Shore ending at Crisfield where oysters were transported for delivery throughout the country. Eventually, the industry shifted to the harvest and packaging of crab meat, which remains important to this community today. Consequently, the town's water tank declares Crisfield to be the "Crab Capital of the World."

While somewhat remote, this town is the site for numerous popular festivals and events. Among these are the J. Millard Tawes Oyster and Bull Roast, an annual Soft Shell Spring Fair, the National Hard Crab Derby and Fair, the annual Skipjack Races and Festival, and a host of others. Check with the local chamber of commerce (410-968-2500) for dates.

## NAVIGATION

In Tangier Sound, the entrance to the Little Annemessex River is marked by Jane's Island Light. The channel leading up the river to Crisfield is well marked and easily navigated. The entrance to the town's harbor is clearly marked to starboard. The harbor is largely occupied by Somers Cove Marina, however, there are also areas suited for anchoring.

Photo Tom Henschel

Restoration of a Skipjack at the
Chesapeake Bay Maritime Museum.
Photo by Laura Vlahovich